ADVANCE PRAISE FOR
Love like a Conflagration

SAMUEL HAZO, past poet laureate of Pennsylvania

Prepare to be impressed. And moved. There is not a poem in this remarkable book that will leave you unchanged or be forgotten. The settings range from hell to the Cafe Pontalba. A lover is addressed passionately: "tell how I take your breath away." There is a dream of an eternal Eden: "There will we also lie like strangers after passion?" There is dalliance: "It is her innocent delight / to think of the man unmet as yet." There is Christ: "Christ the Communist Christ the queer / Christ the many who live to annoy me / Christ the sorry face in my mirror." The language and tone vary from updated Elizabethan to holy slang. As for imagery and rhythm, how can this passage be bettered?—"Astonishments of sparrows / lifted, like bright ideas, / from the red dust of furrows, / giddy with innocence." The author is a woman in full, and each of her poems is as permanently current as it is consummate. She puts on the page the passion long absent from American poetry. I've never read a book as poetically and beautifully frank as this.

JAMES MATTHEW WILSON, poetry editor, *Modern Age*

Jane Greer's poetry is intelligent, profound, and tough, something like an avenging angel, striding into the living room and beating the curio cabinet with his sword until all the porcelain cherubs have been smashed. Technically sound and unsparingly sharp, she helps mark a new age in Catholic letters.

ANTHONY ESOLEN, translator, *The Modern Library Divine Comedy*

These poems by Jane Greer, who has never mistaken formlessness for sophistication or flippancy for wisdom, are works of art—and

I mean that praise in its fullest sense. They are shaped, like the capitals of a Romanesque column, or like the column, or like the church whereof the capital and column are parts—and like the church, they treat of the great range of the human story from Fall to Redemption, never forgetting the sad and beautiful muddle of our lives in between. They are about the world and people in it, and they are meant to be understood and to be appreciated for their precise and varied and exquisite music.

RYAN WILSON, editor, *Literary Matters*

Opening with a thunderously oracular and brilliant modification of the Sapphic strophe—the stanza of antiquity's greatest love poet—Jane Greer's *Love like a Conflagration* gives us the modern world in the crucible of an acutely moral and metaphysical vision. Personal without forsaking wit and plainspoken without forsaking elegance, these poems embody the tension between the desires of this world and the desire for the divine. From seemingly mundane materials—a "red-eyed ferret," a beachball's "lavish noncha-lance" in an empty hotel pool, "a Muzak station," a red-tailed hawk, "the clean bones of cottonwoods"—Greer's art stokes a revelatory blaze. The best of these poems, kindled to life by im-ages available only to the eye of vigilance and fueled by that faith-ful rendering only patience can achieve, speak to us like bonfires in the darkness. Listen, and listen again.

C.C. PECKNOLD, chairman, Academy of Catholic Theology

In some secret corner—nestled between Seamus Heaney's "Death of a Naturalist" and Gerard Manley Hopkins' "As Kingfishers Catch Fire"—there exists the brilliant poetry of Jane Greer. Like the exquisite swoop of a rough-legged hawk, her poems are a se-vere mercy, counseling against despair and breaking the monotony of sin by the fiercest fire of divine charity. Highly rec-ommended.

A.M. JUSTER, poetry editor, *First Things*

Jane Greer's new collection of poems, *Love like a Conflagration*, is masterful. Her work is rooted in her faith, her love of language, her attention to detail, and her wide range of interests. It is also witty and exquisitely crafted—a book you will want to give to a friend after enjoying it yourself.

JENNIFER REESER, author, *Indigent*

There are reasons for Jane Greer's rhyme. Upon opening *Love like a Conflagration*, the reader is immediately introduced to meticulous verse-craft, poetry aware of and in control of itself, by every line. Greer's range is wide and her intellectual curiosity deep, two aspects of her art which are blessedly well-matched by the level of skill with which she is able to treat everything from the most nebulous abstractions to the most concrete of real-world details. This is a book for the eclectic reader, especially, both aca-demic and simple, whom it will leave—in the poet's own words from her sublime "Saved"— "lifted in a moment ... startled, with some subtle feelings, oddly bittersweet: a sense of loss with no re-membered having, of cooling where I hadn't noticed heat."

LOVE LIKE A CONFLAGRATION

Poems by Jane Greer

PITTSBURGH:
Lambing Press, 2020

Acknowledgments. Many of the poems in *Love Like a Conflagration* first appeared in the anthologies *A Formal Feeling Comes* (ed. Annie Finch) and *A Garland for Harry Duncan* (ed. W. Thomas Taylor), and in the journals *America, Angelus, Better Than Starbucks, Black Willow, Chronicles of Culture, Critique, Dakota Arts Quarterly, First Things, In-Sense, Literary Matters, The Lyric, Midwest Poetry Review, Modern Age, Piedmont Literary Review, Plains Poetry Journal, Presence: A Journal of Catholic Poetry, South Coast Poetry Journal,* and *The Yale Literary Magazine.*

Bathsheba on the Third Day (© 1986 Jane Greer) was first published in a limited edition of three hundred copies, hand-set and hand-printed by Harry Duncan at The Cummington Press, courtesy of the University of Nebraska at Omaha College of Fine Arts.

For my husband, Jim Luptak

that look / saying, where did you come from, / how did I get so blessed, / aren't we wonderful

and for Mike Aquilina

this book's godfather

Contents

MICHA-EL

Micha-el

You lull yourselves with dimple-handed cherubs
simpering in your étagère half-naked;
small-breasted maidens, tissue-winged and swooning
there on your desktop;

all those complacent fleshy pastel eunuchs
posing with harp or horn on the Christmas mantel:
you underestimate to your own peril
Whom we have come from,

Whom we are acting for, and it's too late now:
suddenly it's too late to ask for mercy.
Mercy is what you'll get—His wide-armed mercy—
but you won't like it.

He has been with you, at your elbow, lovesick,
down the millennia. He knows you deeply,
yet still encumbers your black hearts with blessings.
Willing unwillful

swain, He has wept and waited while you mocked Him.
Finally, now, the muscles of His jawline
clench and unclench beneath that holy shadow:
Enough is enough.

Don't act as though some game's been played unfairly:
He's never skimped on prophets since He breathed you
out of the mud and on your way to Heaven—
yours for the asking—

but you were too intent on what you'd crawled from.
You can't begin to dream what you've rejected,
what we would give to need His fierce salvation,
require His dying . . . .

Love like a conflagration shall be yours now;
love like an April river, like a temblor;
love like an avalanche, a midnight bomb-blast,
finding you hidden,

shrieking the air with shards of stained-glass windows;
love like a sunstorm, sweeping before it nations,
continents, galaxies, and all your hubris.
Yes, say your prayers now.

This is your Precious Moment, I its angel,
angry and dark and terrible. God With Us,
Emmanu-el, comes bearing yet more mercy,
but you won't like it.

AT THE GARDEN OF
ORGANIC DELIGHT

At the Garden of Organic Delight

Across Royal from Pere Antoine,
slinky young men in black Lycra
lounge in the fragrant doorway, murmur
miss, hey miss, come smell this soap
handmade from salvia, sage, angelica,
hyssop, wormwood, a soupçon of rue.
Here's a free sample if you'll just step inside—
and suddenly, stepping inside is what
I desire, more than anything, to do.

Over Espresso

George Steiner says we're rising towards
a time when we will not need words,
when language will be useless, talk
superfluous, and we will walk
around just sort of *being* love,
you know, with nothing left to prove.

Till then, dear, let us be explicit.
Nothing in making love's illicit,
and nothing pleases like the sound
of one's own virtues rolling round
in someone else's mouth. So *say:*
tell how I take your breath away.

The Adulterer in Hell

Those were enchanted years,
when love was reason enough for love
and dreams were prodigal without remorse.
What was there left to have

save Heaven? We would yield,
but slowly, make delicious Death
court us even as we caught our breath
at the joy Death held.

We were not so young
as to be ungrateful; still, the losses
sifted daily into our stolen kisses,
stone by stone on our tongues.

Where are the *mots justes*
we wrapped our lovely sin in then?
They strike as I recall them, stone by stone,
into my soul's black waste.

All that's left is the Word:
distant, sorrowful beyond measure.
He who is Guest and Host at every pleasure
took our snubbing hard.

At the Center of the Universe

The universe around me spins,
a hot tornado, blurred with speed;
at the still center of the din
am I, with my cold stonelike need
for something I can't seem to name
but used to have, and would reclaim.

The universe around me slows
and stops, as time and space conspire,
while I, the thrashing center, grow
more and more restive with desire
for something I can't seem to name
but used to have, and would reclaim.

Her Green Desire

is thorn and thicket, twisted root,
tangle of shoot and tendril, hot
and wet, everything overmuch,

a wet green Paradise through which
winds whitely (though she cannot hear it),
watery-mouthed, a red-eyed ferret

Rough-legged Hawk

Suddenly she is there,
limned above the budding ash,
riding indifferent air.
Her hunger never ceases.

Patient beyond compare,
when she tilts tail in a white flash,
mouse and man, beware!
Her dominion increases.

Dismissing our despair,
she will keep our hearts in a high cache,
wound with bone and hair,
then tear them to pieces.

Lines on a Plain Brown Wrapper

Sin in its near occasions rises
glad as a long-lost friend, devises
help for tumescent glands and hearts,
deflects our best intent, and starts
along the path of least resistance
all those desires kept at a distance.
It cannot be put off. I try,
all day, to look sin in the eye,
say I will go and sin no more:
the Compleat Coach, sin knows the score.
Should I sin gladly—play sin's game—
or miserably, it's all the same.

How like a Muzak station sin
fashions harmlessness into din,
insinuates itself in shivers
down the broad backs of true believers!
Each soul's dank cellar has at least
one crack through which sin slithers, greased
lightning its tongue, its look concerned
lest we flout pleasure, choose to burn
passively in our lust or pride.
Sin longs to give what we've denied
ourselves, leads us in easy stages
—but makes some bones about its wages.

Ophelia

Here the girl gazes
hard at the water
as it replaces
itself with a shiver.

Over sand, coyly;
around rock, torrential:
all interstitial
rages this river,

holding together
both its banked boundaries
with its pure absence,
with its cold leaving.

All interstitial,
endless departure;
nothing is permanent
but its deceiving.

There is no weight here,
there is no color,
nothing of substance
—shadow and glare—

and yet how solid
seem those deep shadows,
dark underpinnings
not really there.

Last Things

In all that you attempt, you will find success—
no, near-sublimity, save for a flaw
you can't define: the perfection of wax roses.
Somewhere a man who wants your vote next fall

will kiss a tyrant, tour his model prison
(well, most of it). You'll hit your child. The bruise
won't disappear. Straight out of Revelation,
a goose will court a cow for seven years.

Men will make babies any way they want to—
start them in Dixie cups, sell them to various
wombs. When the kids learn what they've gotten into,
preschool Dial-a-Porn won't make them curious.

Fidelity will be an anachronism—
what idiot would tie that knot forever?—
and you will live from spasm to exquisite spasm,
your life a rush, your happiness a quiver.

Then the phone will ring, the caller hang up quietly,
just as you get it on with your neighbor's wife.
You'll check your locks and alarms and revolver nightly,
stock up on scotch and pills, put your jewels in the safe,

yet early some morning—wouldn't you know it!—just
as you pop an oxy, there's that dreaded knock;
He leans on your doorbell, arms full of Bibles. Christ!
Sometimes it seems like you just can't catch a break.

Bourbon, Neat

Thin to a filament of fire and fall,
web of hot wire, down my dark veins,
to bundle me in my blackroot hollow.
What heat you lose, such heart I gain.

Such heart I gain, pale amber swallow,
kindles the bone where you coil and hiss.
Whose supple lover on a silk pillow
seizes the blood in a blaze like this?

Deadline

At water's edge, an avocet
weaves shallow tracks around her worry,
cuneiform in slant light.

Haphazard glyphs her alphabet,
her blood is prodding her to hurry,
finish her work before the night.

Professor Dobbs
to Jayleen Nichols
on Semantics and
the Cold Fact of Myth

. . . Take the word "fall." Out in the garden
two quick souls watch morning harden
over the maidenhair and rue
along the dappled bottoms, grow
impatient at their skins, that keep
pleasure and knowledge just skin-deep.
Gifts to each other, they become
weary of calling Eden home
where passion sleeps, that in them rises
fiercer than either realizes.
And so they cast off innocence,
that hand-me-down worn only once;
they fall, in short, in love, and spend
their new hearts' thunder toward this end:
that death should die. Thus do they earn
—clumsily, time and time again—
freedom that they were freely given:
efforts redundant, but a Heaven
defoliated of desire
moves our fell hunger less than fire.

    Silence. You think me nearly dead

already, harmless, quaint and mad.
Still, you stayed after. Do I dare
harvest the fruit scent of your hair?

Now, in the autumn green things plummet
deathward, toward their earthly limits,
remnants of Paradise undone:
fall turns the vital into stone.
And we, we poor dumb beasts, we try
to weave from waste a victory;
to read, from random sin, direction;
to make from myth a resurrection.

I know like my own sins your wrists'
white undersides, the amethyst
shadows upon that fallen snow,
most subtle source of vertigo.

Should we grow dizzy, spin and fall,
falling is not a sin at all,
my dear; rather, it proves the myth
that we are red in nail and tooth.
Falling will ground us where we lie
looking for immortality,
and in each falling we will rise
to the occasion: our demise.

After the Fall

The sound was everything I'd read it was,
and more: soft and precise,
a single apple dropped on sodden ground.
Now time is measured from that sound.

Not in my ears, but roiling through my marrow
swept a sudden sorrow.
Then the epiphany: sick rushing knowledge
that I had done irreparable damage.

Never again the luxury of ease
or happy thoughtlessness.
So innocent and careless was that life
before! Now the world's unsafe,

the smallest gesture feels as if it matters,
this side of the fracture,
and I consider long where to place my feet—
always aware that it's too late.

I Have Gone Out

Colossians 3:12-14

With these I can often manage to cover myself:
kindness, gentleness, patience, compassion, humility.
This is nothing to boast about—any lifelong pagan,
any blown-adrift secular soul grateful to nothing
can be gentle and humble all day long. In fact,
I learned early to dress up in these virtues
when what counts most is making things run smoothly.

But this is just underclothing, meant to be clean
and seamless, but also meant to be covered richly
with something shining, with some resplendent, new,
absolutely needful, gleaming overgarment
to perfect the entirety: so very needful,
so utterly requisite that merely its absence
renders all those grand virtues not just imperfect
but useless; and not just useless but obscene.

More often than just today and yesterday,
more often than not, I have gone out wearing
all my fine underwear on full display,
quite satisfied with myself; I have gone out
with never a thought of trying to put on love.

Thoughts on Witnessing
a Final Profession
The Rule of St. Benedict, Chapter 72

"I will prefer nothing whatever to Christ,"
she says, and I am plunged deep into wonder
at what that might feel like, that sacrifice,
if I released the things of which I'm fonder
than I am of Christ, it seems: My ease. My pride.
Huge losses, these: my dearest flaws! And yet
take them, sweet Christ. They will not be denied
by trying, but they cause me such regret.
My pride, my comfort: crush them now, I pray.
Take them by force. Destroy them. And be swift.
I prefer you to have them, but each day
I lack the heart to make of them a gift.

Unrequited

Think of what you call us to:
love that mirrors what you do,
loving us for small return
or no return (although we yearn
for what we misperceive as you).
Love, and count it all as loss
you croak, shattered, from your cross.
This is what you call us to?

We're just not that into you.

Great Blue

In the far shallows, still and faint,
the heron waits, all coming storm
and thunder, and yet all restraint.

Waits unquivering, cool, controlled,
for that dark riot of feathered flame
from his still heart wingward to unfold,

wakened by some bone-deep desire.
Three hard strokes of daunting wideness
and he is gone.

IN THE POOL AT THE
BOURBON ORLEANS

In the Pool at the Bourbon Orleans

Behold the empty courtyard with its army
of pristine lounges guarding the empty pool—
empty but for a beach ball trapped, untroubled,
spinning and skimming like a drunken fool,
making Venn diagrams on the water's surface,
skidding and tilting—perhaps randomly,
perhaps not—from edge to travertine edge.
Hold in your mind the glad captivity,
the lavish nonchalance, the willingness
to be blown and batted, possibly ignored,
instructed only by small breaths of wind
in a game that seems to be its own reward:
aimless and fruitless and purposeless, perhaps,
but altogether pleasing to the Lord.

At the Cafe Pontalba

It is quite pleasant at the Cafe Pontalba
in the hot mid-morning, at a window table
(the slow fans, the air thick as water)
here where Chartres crosses St. Peter.

Out there, in the glare of the white cathedral,
life lifts its head. At some subtle signal,
spooled from the alleys, deliberate movement
slides into focus on shimmering pavement.

Hair braiders, drummers, portrait painters,
acrobats, charlatans, shoe shiners, ranters,
henna queens, drag queens, the next Marsalis,
the next Vermeer, the Lucky Dogs seller:

in yesterday's clothes, in sleep-deprived glory—
hungry, hungover, resolute, weary—
today, as every dry day, they return
to carry on. Or to try again.

In here, though, it is cooler, dimmer.
Drive and vocation are simply rumors,
and action seems borderline-indecent.
In the Cafe Pontalba, it is very pleasant.

Saved

It was not until I felt the fever passing
that I realized how ill I'd really been.
I think it must have kindled me in secret
for a long time, like a merely venial sin,
but it lifted in a moment—left me startled,
with some subtle feelings, oddly bittersweet:
a sense of loss with no remembered having,
of cooling where I hadn't noticed heat.

This Blue

The way the light of you
finds me through the hot,
bright unnameable blue,

that square of ancient glass
in the high apse window,
backlit at mid-day Mass:

blue should not feel like burning,
like a blazing lighthouse lamp,
so here I am, learning

this color like a child
too young for words: *this* blue
to seek me, self-exiled;

this blue to find me, hiding;
this blue to hold me, helpless,
in your cool fire abiding.

Just a small shard, this blue,
yet I am pierced and pinned.
For me, today, no *credo*: only you.

On Nearing Our
Thirty-fifth Anniversary

From opposite ends of the couch
we text each other jokes
and outrageous political gaffes
we've found. We each desire
the same reward for our craft:
a head thrown back, a snort,
and, more than anything else—
and every time—that look
saying, where did you come from,
how did I get so blessed,
aren't we wonderful.

The Poet at 80

Here fall the years in furious disorder;
thin pages in her own determined hand
blow like leafmeal along the smoky border
of that dark continent, that motherland
called memory. Daily, parts of her crumble
before her eyes and just beyond her reach;
odd how the recent days are first to tumble,
hard-bound, whole signatures, into the breach.

She learns, by virtue of her new unknowing,
indifference to failure or acclaim;
by increments her swift untimely slowing
sharpens her focus as it dulls her shame,
and, resolute, she works to write a defter
line, a more promising stanza, every day,
grateful for language that has not yet left her,
not yet failed or refused her or blown away.

Ann Gammell, 1909-1982

Think of the red-tailed hawk: she tilts and shines
on unseen axis, fastened to the sun.
Think how she seeks a winghold in the air,
falling a little, rising with bold strokes
above her hunger, nearer perfect vision,
old feats forgotten in brush below.
Fearless she climbs the thinning molecules
in a slow spiral, working her way home,
spilling her sharp cry on this dusty valley.

Think how then with imperceptible leaning
into wind she levels her rapturous wings,
a thin dark thread across our line of sight,
and even as we squint into the blue
she's swept back through a slit hidden in light.

Holy Thursday

Toward the basins and the towels
Christ tonight we shuffle in silence
Christ behind me Christ before me
Christ to help me keep my balance
Christ the unwashed Son of Man
whose pulsing scars live on my wrist
where is a greater mystery
washing each other we wash Christ

Christ the infant sweet from her bath
Christ the eighth-grader wracked with sex
Christ the old woman slowing me down
and the neighbor man who never speaks
Christ the sullen secretary
Christ the star in the limousine
Christ my husband talking with the dog
Christ on the corner selling cocaine

Christ the child in the treehouse crying
Christ her daddy and his bad touch
Christ the losers who do not love me
and also those who love me too much
Christ the young brutes who bully my child
Christ all those who really mean well
Christ the serial killers and senators
and everyone I'm sure will rot in Hell

Christ the invisible Christ the refusable
Christ the runaway under the bridge
Christ the forgettable the insignificant
living in shadow on the edge
Christ the re-tard Christ the hippie
Christ the communist Christ the queer
Christ the many who live to annoy me
Christ the sorry face in my mirror

Admit Impediments

Into the ark of sleep descend our breaths,
small coupled animals. Our several deaths
flung us this evening headlong heavenward, and earth's

finer distinctions between love and sin
perished, too, as the sweet, hard-won
pleasure we labored over came and went. We learn

nothing from non-success, cry out and thrash,
beasts in a snare, to make ourselves one flesh—
as though we really could. Today the priest smudged ash

into our foreheads as we gravely knelt,
admonished us to search ourselves for guilt,
banished us to the garden Second Adam built.

There will we also lie like strangers after passion?
Or will the word be flesh, the flesh forgiven
its driven, unholy hunger? Will I learn who you are in Heaven?

God of the Gold and Purple Finches

Finches at all my feeders flash and bicker
in ritual consternation and all weather,
jangle at me with never-ending want,
need me compliant but omnipotent.
Within the nearby pine, push comes to shove
as the shrill chorus nags me, makes me leave
the cool deck and my chair and drink and book
to fetch seed quickly, fix their rotten luck.
The bounty I bestow with great affection
they apprehend as wanton dereliction,
and no amount of care will bring me love:
their gratitude grows less the more I give.
There's no end to their petulance and hunger.
Their ceaseless praying always sounds like anger
at me, all-kind, all-generous, all-seeing,
in whom they live and move and have their being.

Because God Wanted It

I stood alone in my dark back yard to grieve
uncountable wrongs that I had yet to receive.
What had undone me? Simply that a friend
wronged me in ways she claimed not to intend.
Still, I was Moses, grinding that gold to dust
beneath my righteous heel, my hurt robust
and richly fed. I was a walking bruise,
wandering old, familiar avenues—
so old, and so familiar, and so grim—
my heart's metrics a loud, discordant hymn.
There in the cloudy dark, I shunned the Word:
breakers of pain were what I more preferred,
over and over driven to revisit
our every utterance and each exquisite
pause and riposte. My pique was blackest yes:
yes to the Devil's thoughtful, hot caress,
yes to some fracture that might not be mended.
I stoked my little hurt to hate most splendid
and in that fever found surpassing pleasure
too urgent to rebuke, too rich to measure—
downfall that very nearly felt devout

—then the clouds parted and the moon came out,
large and unsparing, full in my livid face:
substantiation of a saving grace.
Raise a doxology to that brisk shake,

that light whose suddenness knocked me awake,
delivered me embroiled in sin's commission.
I had not prayed, did not yet feel contrition,
was not yet sorry, humbled, or ashamed:
in the very act of straying, I was claimed.
Because God wanted it, because God could,
because God loves me with my speck of good,
because the Holy Spirit over the bent
world broods, I was redeemed impenitent.

Old Dog

Her food and water live across the room.
She has a thought. She lifts her nose. She measures
and weighs effort and risk, her hunger's bloom,
the long, slick floor between her and her pleasures,

and then decides. Long stretches—fore, then hind—
and she sets off, her stiff legs under control,
eyes on the prize, just one thing on her mind.
Listing only slightly, she reaches the goal

—and then just stands there, rueful and perplexed,
inches from Paradise without a clue.
She sits. She stares at the wall, not sure what's next,
how she has come there, what she had meant to do.

As It Turns Out

Give me, I thought, a stand of tilted pines
guarding white water hurtling into mist.
Give me a steep-cut torrent over stones,
trout-bright, clear and fast.

Or better, I wished, give me the reckless reach
of a winter sea, heaved by moon and wind,
salt-sweet mayhem roaring across a beach's
apron of frosted sand.

But that was long ago. Instead, these plains
remained my home, their waters slow and deep
and muddy, their gritty wind pockmarking plans,
fraying our early hopes.

None of that matters, for in you I have found,
across the decades, water deep and still
enough to fill me, and shelter from the wind
such as makes wind worthwhile.

In the Hot Courtyard

On all of us there was such dust,
in all of us such bickering thirst,
and there was a secret—undiscussed,
unrecognized, and about to burst.

She touched his shoulder as we waited
thirsty as hell. He frowned. He balked.
But *yes* was transubstantiated,
water to wine, as we talked.

BATHESHEBA ON THE THIRD DAY

One

In the Beginning

In the beginning, there was next to nothing:
dark still undreamed-of, dark's bright wake unflowing,
time an unlanguaged name for massive, grinding
dreams of I Am.

Then a vast waking cleft the world forever.
First the glad darkness, like an undammed river,
then the shy light, gifts of the world's first lover,
tender I Am.

Out of this merging dark and light a garden
grew in God's palm; He saw that it was good and
coaxed with His breath the clay to free the sudden
son of I Am.

Softly, shy Adam trod the fecund valleys,
parting with patient, dumb dismay each willow's
sticky, red-nippled hair to no avail. O,
back to I Am,

sap-struck and all unstrung with nameless wanting,
stumbled poor Adam: puzzled, swollen, panting.
Pensive, as though He knew what might be coming,
kindly I Am

kindled from Adam's bone a white-coiled, wakened
Eve, with her buds all apple-blush. Thus quickened
happy inventiveness they had not reckoned—
nor had I Am.

Sorrowfully, He saw them take Him lightly,
squandering nights and days most indiscreetly;
love was their only liturgy, devoutly
void of I Am,

He Who had fashioned love to His Own glory!
Why such betrayal? Flung in God's first fury
out of the garden, Adam answered softly,
Because I Am.

Two

Pastoral

There is a primly tended park
where, in the noon sun, shadows quiver;
there is a muddy blood-warm river
murmuring lies from dark to dark;
and, in between, a snarl of grass
the mowing man, in the heat, forgot.
Knee-deep, waist-deep, steaming in hot
sun, it lets no lovers pass.

Young men and women shed their clothes
without relief among the trees:
ardor is dampened by degrees.
But in the long grass something grows
importunate of appetite
and roots its deepest self in mire,
waiting for those whose fresh desire
will fell them, fell them, come the night.

Traveling from
There to Here

Every hawk in the world
hung above that highway,
hunting between gnarled
knuckles of hill and the sky.

Astonishments of sparrows
lifted, like bright ideas,
from the red dust of furrows,
giddy with innocence.

Granting no time for fear,
hawks, with sudden seizure,
bred in the bloody air
a darker pleasure.

Rodin's *Gates of Hell*

This is too tall, dark wave of soul
tossed molten up against the wall,
blown out from some vile secret hole,
sinners spit from the bilge of Hell,
half-melted in fire where time has frozen.
Starved for the firm flesh of his child,
Ugolino in highest treason
breaks his fast but is never filled,
love eating love, time out of time.
Back-to-back, bronze unrelenting
lovers suffer, their once-sublime
bodies grown muscle-bound with wanting.
Paolo and Francesca fall
eternally though they cling and clamber,
lust and unfaithfulness their pall,
passion their torture to remember.
Torsos and arms I somehow know
are thrust, broken, from the black gulf;
heads of the damned emerge from shadow,
ghosts of all sorrow, of myself.
Shades in each other's shadows quicken;
by their sad breath the bronze is tarnished.
Still, great unpeopled breakers beckon.
This is too large. And too unfinished.

That Woman

She wraps herself
in secret circles taut as wire
and fine as fear,
turning his uncomplex desire
into a web
of geometrics puzzled, grim,
tangled as hair.
She circumscribes herself with him,
he unaware.

All day she dreams,
painting hot bands across her throat,
his hungry mouth.
His words like music note by note
bind her. She dreams
he watches as she climbs the stair;
his eyes approve.
She rarefies the merely rare:
a good man's love.

His honest needs
and passion are the boundary
her circles seek.
She reads her own reality
from his rough hands.

Her dream's the same asleep, awake,
alone or wed:
she needs a simple man to make
her subtle bed.

The Romantic

He has no face—yet his face hangs
dark as an apple in her dreams.
This is the miracle, she thinks,
oh, twice each minute, as she works
(halfheartedly) at keeping busy,
or seeming to: how easily
he makes her happy, though she's never
seen him: her next and unmet lover.

John is a dear: she couldn't find
anyone sweeter, and she's fond
of him and his attentiveness:
"Made to be married," he always says.
But things can be *too* cozy: John
could spend each blessed night at home
with her and the ticking clock, and not
hear the world wild with all regret.

It is her innocent delight
to think of the man unmet as yet:
how he will first admire her mind
(John does, but doesn't understand
how to be, well, *fierce* about it):
then he'll arrange for them to "meet":
the look on his stricken face will show
his eggs are in one basket now.

Maybe *he's* married, too; they could
deny the rude surging of their blood
for long, delicious months, suffer
gladly their secret pain, and offer
daily, each one, to call it off.
That's *almost* nicer than sweaty love,
and, really, who does it hurt? But then
he'll grow impatient, take her in hand,

show her how desperate he is.
(John won't even be curious
about her afternoons at the lake.
Poor John.) The two of them will drink
each other greedily, in shadowed
rooms where such things are allowed,
fingers and tongues harass and claw
cruelly, cruelly, cruelly ... *now.*

And so she is happy. Well, she *is.*
—It's just that when she sees John's face
content above his morning paper,
she feels ... not kept, but like his keeper.
Still, she is hot and ripe, and harvest
claims all fruit which hasn't burst—
harvest only a kinder name
for that ticking sound in the evening.

Foxtrot

The dance instructor, dressed in red,
tossed her page-boy, cocked her head,
winked, and warned them not to touch
just yet. "Touching," she said, "is much
too dangerous to try until
you know what you are doing." Still,
off with her partner she swung, four
legs moving as two, a score
of envious eyes ogling their fused
pivoting pelvises: he amused,
she intent. Abruptly her ardor
broke and, breathing a little harder,
she pushed away in vague distress,
with sidelong glances, smoothed her dress
(that dancing thing), and leaned once more
to the eager class on the chessboard floor.

A Sort of Parable

Lemon and lavender and ash-white:
thousands of butterflies hung low
and thick, a comforter of light
smoothed across the vacant lot,
heavy upon the waist-high grass.
A lovely shortcut, Prudence thought,
and entered, leading with her heart.
Then all the butterflies at once
lifted and plied their maddest art,
assaulting poor Prue as she passed,
clinging in clouds to her pale face,
wild arms and hair, a shadow cast
in color, fervent flying ocean.
And Prudence fled. All she had wanted
was a quick trip, not such emotion.

Feminist Androgyne

After "Androgyny," a composite photograph by Nancy Burson, formed
by feeding photographs of six men and six women, selected at random,
into a computer programmed to merge facial features

Here on this page I am poured out like water,
child of (times six) my father and my mother,
fruit of adulterated seed, blurred daughter,
born unregenerate: your long-dreamed lover.

Prophet and ghost and cipher, I was made
most digitally: my parents put their heads
together: input, output, I was laid,
pure printout from their cold collective beds.

No vague hermaphrodite, I wrench your breath,
rally those old misshapen, desperate dreams
you thought you'd shed. New snakeskin (sweet false death!),
they grow back stronger, garment without seams.

Charismatic, mine is a tongue not human;
like smoke or an ill-healed scar, my smudge of hair.
I wear few shadows—yet am wholly woman.
Does that astonish you? Look, if you dare,

you who gaze in a mirror and go blind.
Satan, Adam, Eve in her new-fleshed power:
I am more than kin, my dear, and less than kind:
what wouldn't you give to have me for an hour!

Bathsheba
on the Third Day

Hot, hot, hot
is all those spooky crows
can think to say. We ought
to have some people over,
take in a funny show,
redecorate this tent.
Aren't you listening, lover?
We'll just have to invent
our own fun, take a course,
maybe, in the fall, and then . . .
Oh, please, babe, not *again*!
We never *talk* any more.

Three

Heartwounding Woods

Do you recall the late-afternoon light
oblique in October woods, the slanting gold
carelessly cast, mottling the secret ground?
The smoke of dreams surrendered or attained
hung in the air, and loss and discontent
grew in the still-green dappled undergrowth.
Do you remember, deep in heartwounding woods,
pungent longing in the pungent leaves
as you sat in stippled shade with half-closed eyes
and there moved across your face and toward the night
the last patch of irretrievable light?

Ghost Story

It was that time of deep late summer
when ripe the silence hangs sweet-fleshed,
that hour of light's most brief, most lavish
spilling of self through the orchard's wicker

before it fails. I in my harvest
of dry white paper, in my high room,
my woods of books, heard the child's voice chime
in the field beyond my darkfruit forest.

Rising, I saw her, wide-armed whirling
in the light's last pulse behind the trees:
sneakered, laughing, solitary:

glimpse of brown leg, flash of bright hair,
a shade's abandon, ghost's grace—
cruel haste to leave me though I called her.

Without, Within

The wind moves tonight
among wet alder
wantoning their leaves
as their roots grow colder.

High moon, high moon
above my slick roof
makes a single shadow
substantial grief.

Cranes mourn and murmur
in high-flung flocks
as I put passion away
in a cedar box.

The Haunting

When struck, timbre of heartwood; heft of stone
when weighed; uneasy wrapping of cold flesh
not flesh across your back: each more than wish,
less than desire, leaving you unalone
in singular camaraderie of grief.
These ghosts walk through no walls, hurl no book
to your floor, startle you most in your own look
sometimes from a mirror; your bed is safe
so long as you sleep. No wisps of ether, they:
solid as smoke sweet in a blaze of October,
thick as the scent of April under cover
of late intractable March. Hard company,
they grow young in your old age, they mean to stay,
these ghosts of love you never gave away.

Couplets

Walk a black boulevard through flame
this sharp October. Speak my name

to the flesh made dust, the clean bones
of cottonwoods. Let small wet stones

frosted with lichen lead you down
to the sky turning the river brown.

Speak my name, look up, and see
gulls engaged in their savagery

over the pewter water, small
stubborn hearts in a bright squall.

Kick the dry leaves as if they matter,
making them suffer as they scatter;

hang on the air stiff mists of breath
borrowed to be returned at death.

Twice Betrayed

See my winding sheet
sloughed like a skin of scales,
four days' dust at my feet
foul as entrails.

Take away the stone
cut like a sword into me:
back through Hell I was blown
violently.

Now I know what I've read
these years in your speechless eyes:
the easy bones of the dead
tell only lies.

Unbind him, and let him go
—as if we had reached an end.
Do you love me enough, old friend,
to make it so?

Coda

Long lines of birds in the bone sky
tilt and dip and plunge me to the heart;
I will be leaving more of myself
on this dark bridge over the frozen river
than I like, more than longing can restore.

Under the ice the black river rushes on
into the arms of some spring I cannot see;
this guardrail spins and grows confused
where fingers have touched and leapt apart
for all the world as if the ice were fire.

The birds cry cleanly and straight-heartedly,
cry and are driven; below, a finger of mist
captures and binds in delicate tracery
everything cold, everything dead,
everything left behind but never shed.

The Hunter

Deep in his muddy memory, something makes
a ripple on the smallest space of thick
and enigmatic water, something breaks
a thin stiff shaft of reed, grazes a stick
with wing or fin, disturbs the mist. He wakes.
The pre-dawn clamor in the fluent air
cannot drown out the subtle sound that aches
in his hollow cattail bones and rattles there.

What could it be—this sound of rushing where
there are no wings, this snap of twig in rain,
startling in the eye's white corner, hair
rising on the arms again and again?
Nothing. An absence. Losses beyond repair,
forfeitures, soft arms that would not stay
warm while he learned what early cold he could bear.
The sounds he hears are the ones that got away.

Sweetbriar Dam to the West

Late mad winds race south along the river,
dragging their dark burden of plum and bruised peach.
A gash of white light on the west horizon,
steady and ominous though the sun is falling,
welds these spurting clouds to some distant pasture:
the fine light at the limits of two darknesses,
the bright end of the world over Sweetbriar Dam.

On this cold hill I walk with my coat open,
hands in pockets, ice of my breath blown back at me.
The full moon hidden, I am a windblown maiden
watching her lover's ship break like a wafer on the rocks,
or contemplating death for love of some black-haired stranger;
I am Penelope, spinning, unspinning; Isolde, arms full of death;
I grow larger even than the heart's inventiveness;

yet not so very far below me, indistinct in the near-dusk,
in chiaroscuro of wild cloud, the dun and silent plain
spreads in prosaic barrenness its chaff of shadows,
shrugs itself always westward, taking me prisoner on this hill,
crawls toward the light, falls off the world at Sweetbriar Dam.

You, Standing There,

Small blossoms in your hand
torn from a blooming limb
at river's edge: what grand
passion informed your whim?
Flick of the wrist, unplanned,
and blooms fell to the sand,
sweet luster all struck dim.

White blossoms will not bend
beneath your willful touch,
but, brittle, break, descend
to the white sand—and such
fallings will never mend.
How little noise at the end!
How little, and how much.

Pandora

Dear, you could not have known the harm you courted,
running your small hand over that jar
and needing to hold and have, as children do,
whatever lay hidden away inside;

and you could not have known the harm you wrought,
lifting that lovely painted lid
and loosing all that horror and all that hurt
while the world slept and the old gods groaned;

and you could not be expected to think of the harm
as, most innocent of silly young girls,
dazzled and frightened by your own audacity,
breathless, trying to make things right,

you quickly capped the nearly empty jar
and hope, oldest of curses, most winsome, most patient,
was trapped, caught in that moldy vessel
where still it crouches on some immortal shelf.

Four

Full Circle

The silver undersides of leaves
hide from the sun, but the wind weaves
such perilous textures of the air
silver is caught, now here, now there,
warmed, undone. Slow with suspense,
smoke lifts its flameless abstinence
into a warm wind moving east.
Beauty is waylaid by the beast
before she knows it; his hard flesh
will first repulse and then refresh
her forsworn sensibilities,
hard-pressed under the silvered leaves.

Incense

With this I fill the air between us—
hard to breathe as fire or water—
and miles and years grow longer, straighter,
unwound perimeter of loss.

See how my hand makes a late decision,
lights the stick which burns to ash,
slow as comprehension, slow as flesh
falling in solitary passion.

I fill familiar rooms with currents
redolent of nothing that you are,
and still you make your slow appearance,
uncurl like smoke from my thin despair:
ghost of the undead, scent in air,
I gladder than such vapor warrants.

Lesson Learned on a Long Walk

Tonight there is a ring around the moon
(as it reclines in ice, a pale sliver)
so big the moon is halfway up the sky
and still the circle touches ridge and river.
Look at the circle and it disappears;
paleness and deepness mingle and diffuse.
Look at the moon, the circle calms itself.
To renounce does not always mean to lose.

Better Advice to Colonel Valentine

After Robert Graves

So you are old enough to be her father,
her father's father? Think: does it really matter
that she doesn't know those old songs? Wouldn't you rather

she burn, though briefly, for your admiration,
grow clumsy with love, in exquisite confusion
lay before you her raw sophistication,

than find you *sweet*—or, worse, invisible?
Zounds, man! You *move* her. Can't you see that's all
that counts? Why seek the sad in the essential?

And who's to say this passion's "scarcely decent"?
The fearless heart's hair-triggered; we invent
love, every time we fall, from our urgent present.

If the girl imperils you, laugh at her once,
watch her evaporate. But if a glance
gladdens you both, if the trophies of romance—

the red-hot wire in the bowels, the joyous grief,
the loss in every choice—please you both,
court her with dignity. It may save your life.

Found Poem

I. Catechism

What are the sacraments? The visible
and outward signs of inward grace
(the swift lightening of a loved face,
the cup of wine, the hints of Heaven),
offered by Christ as unassailable
means by which that grace is given.

What is grace? God's goodness towards us,
unearned, undeserved. By grace God grants
our sins' forgiveness, stills our wild wants,
our hungers' bedlam, brims full our common eye,
nurtures our wills; by grace rewards us
for that small good we have ever yet to try.

II.

I think of you, late this long-shadowed afternoon,
nursing your pipe, perhaps, in the close half-dark
of your hot apartment under the pine
as Ann does the dishes quietly. Some thick book
lies in your lap unread, and you are struck
by that introspective indolence you savor.
You plot to change, late this misspent June,

to quit the sad retracing of old designs:
the cosmic and quotidian endeavor.

An old friend said you were forgiven,
asking of you forgiveness also.
You were silent. You were angry.
But we must make what little Heaven
we can manage in our dank souls;
the wind comes up too soon, the dark falls
swift the last few feet, and hungry
beasts our vincible borders prowl.

You have my letter now, and it doesn't matter
whether you answer. Sit where the breeze comes in,
or walk in your calm deliberation down the stairs,
into the street, round the neighborhood all spattered
with light and shadow, unkempt with small affairs
unfinished, busy with ordinary human sin.
I know you love all this, the way familial clatter
and falling dark and sudden rising wind
seem to pay you no heed; here you, invisible
now in the meshed light of these open doors,
alien, see the world inviolable,
all of a piece save for your vague remorse.
Such needless sadness. Words
may mean no more than coquetries of birds
uneasy in the shrubs, but there are hints of Heaven here
dark cannot cover, wind cannot tear.

Falling Awake

A certain dark familiarity
in your smooth back eases the sleep from me
as we roll in unison around the curve
of our short night. Upon the world we carve
our deep initials in this honest fashion:
first by the silence of our slow-limbed passion,
then by our firm abandonment to sleep.
Outside the scope of our intent, the shape
of things to come is hardened by the light;
yet where we lie, knowledge is always night,
bound by our breathing, purposeful and even.
We make our world. We live in very Heaven.

Song of the Passerby

Lovers make their own light
darkly with their breath,
tonguing out some shining,
clinging shibboleth.
As they lie divining
little dawns all night,
bent upon hope,
lovers grope
for a small death of death.

Lovers cast their own dark
lightly all around them.
Stumbling onto lovers,
leave them as you found them:
murmuring under covers,
urgent in the park,
what they find,
keening, unkind,
seems to astound them.